Snap books™

Fun Food for Cool Cooks

Reindeer CRUNCH

AND OTHER CHRISTMAS RECIPES

by Kristi Johnson

Capstone press®

Mankato, Minnesota

Snap Books are published by Capstone Press,
151 Good Counsel Drive, P.O. Box 669, Mankato, Minnesota 56002.
www.capstonepub.com

Library of Congress Cataloging-in-Publication Data
Johnson, Kristi.
    Reindeer crunch and other christmas recipes / by Kristi Johnson.
    p. cm. — (Snap books. Fun food for cool cooks)
    Includes bibliographical references and index.
    Summary: "Provides fun and unique recipes for Christmas including reindeer crunch, triple
chocolate fudge, and gumdrop soda pop cupcakes. Includes easy instructions and a helpful tools glossary
with photos" — Provided by publisher.
    ISBN-13: 978-1-4296-2017-8 (hardcover)
    ISBN-10: 1-4296-2017-X (hardcover)
    1. Christmas cookery — Juvenile literature. I. Title. II. Series.
TX739.2.C45J64 2009
641.5'686 — dc22   2008001762

Editor: Kathryn Clay
Designer: Juliette Peters
Photo Stylist: Sarah L. Schuette

Photo Credits:
All principle photography in this book by Capstone Press/Karon Dubke
Capstone Press/TJ Thoraldson Digital Photography, cooking utensils (all)
Tami Johnson, 32

Capstone Press thanks Kathy Peters for her help with the preparation of this book.

PAGE 14

PAGE 18

PAGE 22

PAGE 24

PAGE 26

TABLE OF CONTENTS

INTRODUCTION

SEEING STARS

When choosing a recipe, let the stars be your guide. Just follow this chart to find recipes that fit your cooking comfort level.

EASY: ★ ☆ ☆
MEDIUM: ★ ★ ☆
ADVANCED: ★ ★ ★

Christmas is full of traditions. Some families go caroling, while others decorate Christmas trees and bake delicious treats. With this book, you'll get tons of ideas to start your own holiday traditions. After a night of caroling, warm up with mugs of Holiday Hot Cocoa. Decorate your tree with Gingerbread Cookie Ornaments. As you open gifts, pass around a plate filled with Triple Chocolate Fudge and Candy Cane Bark. No matter what traditions you celebrate, these recipes are sure to put you in a festive mood.

METRIC CONVERSION GUIDE

United States	Metric
¼ teaspoon	1.2 mL
½ teaspoon	2.5 mL
1 teaspoon	5 mL
1 tablespoon	15 mL
¼ cup	60 mL
⅓ cup	80 mL
½ cup	120 mL
⅔ cup	160 mL
¾ cup	175 mL
1 cup	240 mL
1 quart	1 liter
1 ounce	30 grams
2 ounces	55 grams
4 ounces	110 grams
½ pound	225 grams
1 pound	455 grams

Fahrenheit	Celsius
325°	160°
350°	180°
375°	190°
400°	200°
425°	220°
450°	230°

All good cooks know that a successful recipe takes a little preparation. Use this handy checklist to save time when working in the kitchen.

BEFORE YOU BEGIN

READ YOUR RECIPE

Once you've chosen a recipe, carefully read over it. Everything will go smoothly if you understand the steps and skills.

CHECK THE PANTRY

Make sure you have all the ingredients on hand. After all, it's hard to bake cookies without sugar.

DRESS FOR SUCCESS

Wear an apron to keep your clothes clean. Roll up long sleeves. Tie long hair back so it doesn't get in your way — or in the food.

GET OUT YOUR TOOLS

Sort through the cupboards and gather all the tools you'll need to prepare the recipe. Can't tell a spatula from a mixing spoon? No problem. Refer to the handy tools glossary in this book.

PREPARE YOUR INGREDIENTS

A little prep time at the start will pay off in the end.

- Rinse any fresh ingredients such as fruit and vegetables.
- Use a peeler to remove the peel from foods like apples and carrots.
- Cut up fresh ingredients as called for in the recipe. Keep an adult nearby when using a knife to cut or chop food.
- Measure all the ingredients and place them in separate bowls or containers so they're ready to use. Remember to use the correct measuring cups for dry and wet ingredients.

PREHEAT THE OVEN

If you're baking treats, it's important to preheat the oven. Cakes, cookies, and breads bake better in an oven that's heated to the correct temperature.

The kitchen may be unfamiliar turf for many young chefs. Here's a list of trusty tips to help you keep safe in the kitchen.

KITCHEN SAFETY

ADULT HELPERS

Ask an adult to help. Whether you're chopping, mixing, or baking, you'll want an adult nearby to lend a hand or answer questions.

FIRST AID

Keep a first aid kit handy in the kitchen, just in case you have an accident. A basic first aid kit contains bandages, a cream or spray to treat burns, alcohol wipes, gauze, and a small scissors.

WASH UP

Before starting any recipe, be sure to wash your hands. Wash your hands again after working with messy ingredients like jelly or syrup.

HANDLE HABITS

Turn handles of cooking pots toward the center of the stove. You don't want anyone to bump into a handle that's sticking off the stove.

USING KNIVES

It's always best to get an adult's help when using knives. Choose a knife that's the right size for your hands and the food. Hold the handle firmly when cutting, and keep your fingers away from the blade.

COVER UP

Always wear oven mitts or use pot holders to take hot trays and pans out of the oven.

KEEP IT CLEAN

Spills and drips are bound to happen in the kitchen. Wipe up messes with a paper towel or clean kitchen towel to keep your workspace tidy.

What do Santa's reindeer snack on when they fly around the world? Reindeer Crunch, of course. Mix up some of this trail mix for your own holiday traveling.

DIFFICULTY LEVEL: ★ ★ ★
SERVING SIZE: 8
PREHEAT OVEN: 250° FAHRENHEIT

REINDEER CRUNCH

WHAT YOU NEED

•• *Ingredients*

2 (3.5-ounce) bags unbuttered
    microwave popcorn
1 cup (2 sticks) butter
2 cups brown sugar
½ cup light corn syrup
1 teaspoon salt
½ teaspoon baking soda
1 teaspoon vanilla extract
1 cup dry roasted peanuts
2 cups thin stick pretzels
1 cup dried cranberries
1 cup raisins
1 cup candy coated chocolates

•• *Tools*

roasting pan   saucepan   wooden spoon

oven mitt   pot holder   mixing spoon

nonstick cooking spray

1 Make two bags of microwave popcorn according to package directions. Spray a roasting pan with nonstick cooking spray. Spread out popcorn in the roasting pan.

2 In a small saucepan, melt butter on medium heat. When butter has melted, stir in brown sugar, corn syrup, and salt with a wooden spoon.

3 Turn the burner to high and stir until boiling. Once mixture is boiling, reduce heat to medium and simmer 5 minutes, stirring occasionally.

4 Remove saucepan from heat. Stir in baking soda, vanilla, and peanuts. Pour mixture over the popcorn and mix well with the wooden spoon.

5 Bake caramel corn for 1 hour. Use oven mitts or pot holders to remove the pan every 15 minutes to stir ingredients.

6 Allow caramel corn to cool before breaking it into small pieces. Add pretzels, cranberries, raisins, and candy coated chocolates to the caramel corn and stir with a mixing spoon.

All of the Other Reindeer

Reindeer became part of the Christmas tradition when they appeared in the 1823 poem "A Visit From St. Nicholas." The poem lists Dasher, Dancer, Prancer, Vixen, Comet, Cupid, Donder (not Donner), and Blitzen. Rudolph wasn't introduced until 1939.

For your holiday party, offer guests more than cookies and sweets. An appetizer is the perfect choice. With green and red colors, this dip is a festive and flavorful snack.

DIFFICULTY LEVEL: ★ ☆ ☆
SERVING SIZE: 8

CHRISTMAS DIP

WHAT YOU NEED

•• Ingredients

1 (8-ounce) package cream cheese
1 red bell pepper
1 green bell pepper
¼ cup mayonnaise
2 tablespoons French dressing
2 teaspoons hot sauce
1¼ teaspoons dried parsley flakes
½ teaspoon pepper
½ teaspoon garlic powder
1 teaspoon onion powder
1½ tablespoons Italian seasoning

•• Tools

cutting board

paring knife

mixing bowl

rubber scraper

plastic wrap

1 Allow cream cheese to soften at room temperature for 30 minutes.

2 On a cutting board, cut each bell pepper in half with a paring knife. Scoop out seeds and throw away. Cut half of each pepper into small pieces. Cut the remaining pepper halves into thick strips.

3 In a mixing bowl, combine cream cheese, mayonnaise, French dressing, and hot sauce. Stir the mixture with a rubber scraper until smooth.

4 Add parsley, pepper, garlic powder, onion powder, Italian seasoning, and chopped bell peppers to the mixing bowl. Stir ingredients together with the rubber scraper.

5 Cover bowl with plastic wrap and refrigerate for 1 hour before serving.

6 Serve with bell pepper strips, crackers, sourdough bread, or other veggies.

Make Cleanup a Snap

Don't want to spend a lot of time cleaning up? Serve this dip in a round loaf of sourdough bread. Cut the top off the loaf. Scoop out the soft bread inside until the loaf is hollow. Rip the inside pieces into chunks. Pour the dip into the hollowed-out bread loaf. Spread the bread chunks around the outside of the bread bowl. Best of all, there are no dirty dishes.

It wouldn't be Christmas without cookies. Spritz cookies are a favorite Christmas treat. While most spritz recipes require a special cookie press, you won't need special tools for these.

DIFFICULTY LEVEL: ★ ★ ☆
MAKES: 2 DOZEN COOKIES
PREHEAT OVEN: 350° FAHRENHEIT

SPRITZ STICKS

WHAT YOU NEED

●● Ingredients

1 cup (2 sticks) butter
¾ cup sugar
1 egg
1 teaspoon vanilla extract
¼ teaspoon salt
2¼ cups flour
colored sugar

●● Tools

mixing bowl

electric mixer

small bowl

baking sheet

rolling pin

fork

oven mitt

pot holder

pizza cutter

spatula

wire cooling rack

1 In a mixing bowl, combine butter and sugar. Use an electric mixer on medium speed to cream ingredients together.

2 Crack egg into a small bowl and throw away the shell. Add egg, vanilla, and salt to the mixing bowl. Mix ingredients together with the mixer.

3 Add flour to the mixing bowl. With the mixer on low speed, blend in flour.

4 Place half the dough on an ungreased baking sheet. With a rolling pin, flatten the dough until it is ½-inch thick.

5 Make lines in the dough with a fork. Sprinkle colored sugar over the dough.

6 Bake for 15–20 minutes. Use oven mitts or pot holders to remove baking sheet from the oven.

7 While cookies are warm, use a pizza cutter to cut cookies into strips. Cut strips into small rectangles. With a spatula, place cookies on a wire cooling rack. Repeat steps 4–7 with remaining dough.

Cookie Craze

People around the world celebrate Christmas by baking cookies. Spritz is a popular Christmas cookie in the United States. In Germany, people make *lebkuchen*, a cookie similar to gingerbread. Crunchy, cinnamon cookies called *speculass* are eaten in the Netherlands. Swedish families make *pepparkakor*, a rolled ginger cookie.

13

You don't need lots of ingredients to make a tasty treat. This recipe combines just two classic Christmas ingredients. Mix them together for an easy holiday sweet.

DIFFICULTY LEVEL: ★ ☆ ☆
SERVING SIZE: 8

CANDY CANE BARK

WHAT YOU NEED

Ingredients

10 regular candy canes
2 pounds almond bark

Tools

baking sheet

rolling pin

microwave-safe bowl

wooden spoon

wax paper
zip-top plastic bag

1 Line the bottom of a baking sheet with wax paper.

2 Unwrap candy canes and put them in a zip-top plastic bag. Use a rolling pin to crush candy canes into small pieces.

3 In a microwave-safe bowl, melt almond bark according to package directions. Stop every 30 seconds and stir with a wooden spoon.

4 When almond bark is melted, stir in crushed candy canes.

5 With the wooden spoon, spread a thin layer of the mixture onto the baking sheet. Allow mixture to set for 45 minutes.

6 When candy is hard, break into small pieces.

Tasty Tip

For another fun flavor, replace the almond bark with semisweet chocolate chips. Or use half almond bark and half chocolate chips for a combination of great flavors.

Seeing Stripes

The first candy canes were made in the 1600s. Originally, candy canes were all white. The red stripes didn't appear until the early 1900s. Some believe candy canes are curved to look like shepherds' hooks. Each year, more than 1.7 billion candy canes are made and sold.

15

Decorate your Christmas tree with ornaments that really are good enough to eat. Start with basic gingerbread cookies, and use frosting to make each ornament unique.

DIFFICULTY LEVEL: ★ ★ ☆
MAKES: 1 DOZEN COOKIES
PREHEAT OVEN: 350° FAHRENHEIT

GINGERBREAD COOKIE ORNAMENTS

WHAT YOU NEED

●● *Ingredients*

½ cup sugar
½ cup molasses
⅓ cup vegetable oil
¼ cup hot water
1 egg
½ teaspoon baking soda
½ teaspoon cinnamon
½ teaspoon ground ginger
3 cups flour
2 tablespoons flour, for dusting
colored frosting in a tube

●● *Tools*

mixing bowl   electric mixer   small bowl   rolling mat

rolling pin   cookie cutters   baking sheet

oven mitt   pot holder   spatula

wire cooling rack

plastic wrap
drinking straw
ribbon

1. In a mixing bowl, combine sugar, molasses, vegetable oil, and hot water. Blend ingredients together with an electric mixer on medium speed.

2. Crack egg into a small bowl and throw away shell. Add egg, baking soda, cinnamon, ginger, and flour to mixing bowl. Combine ingredients with the mixer on low speed until dough forms, about 2 minutes. Cover dough in plastic wrap and refrigerate for 1 hour.

3. Sprinkle 2 tablespoons flour on a rolling mat. Place dough on the rolling mat. With a rolling pin, flatten the dough until it is ¼-inch thick.

4. Use cookie cutters to cut fun shapes into the dough. Place cookies on a baking sheet. Use a drinking straw to poke a hole in the top of each cookie.

5. Bake for 10–11 minutes. Use oven mitts or pot holders to remove pan from the oven. With a spatula, place cookies on a wire cooling rack. Let cookies cool for 20 minutes. Decorate with colored frosting.

6. Thread ribbon through the holes and tie loose ends together. Ornaments stay fresh for about 1 week.

A Sweet Treat

People have been making and eating gingerbread cookies since the 1500s. Gingerbread was one of the first cookies associated with Christmas. Now, gingerbread ranges from soft cakes to crispy gingersnaps. People also make gingerbread houses. Some of the fanciest gingerbread houses are found in Nuremberg, Germany, the gingerbread capital of the world.

Does someone on your Christmas list have a sweet tooth? Wrap up a batch of Triple Chocolate Fudge for a gift they're sure to enjoy.

DIFFICULTY LEVEL: ★ ★ ☆
MAKES: 10 PIECES

TRIPLE CHOCOLATE FUDGE

WHAT YOU NEED

● ● *Ingredients*

1 (7-ounce) jar marshmallow creme
1½ cups sugar
⅔ cup evaporated milk
¼ cup butter
½ teaspoon salt
2 cups milk chocolate chips
1 cup semisweet chocolate chips
1 teaspoon vanilla extract
½ cup candy coated chocolates

● ● *Tools*

8 x 8 baking pan

saucepan

wooden spoon

wax paper

1 Line an 8 x 8 baking pan with wax paper.

2 In a large saucepan, combine marshmallow creme, sugar, evaporated milk, butter, and salt. Mix ingredients together with a wooden spoon.

3 Heat on medium until mixture begins to boil, stirring constantly.

4 Once the mixture begins to boil, cook an additional 5 minutes. Continue to stir mixture.

5 Remove the saucepan from heat. Add chocolate chips and vanilla to the saucepan. Stir mixture with the wooden spoon until smooth.

6 Pour mixture into the baking pan. Sprinkle candy coated chocolates on top of mixture.

7 Put the pan into the refrigerator for at least 2 hours or until chocolate is firm. Cut into small squares.

Fudge Facts

Mackinac Island, Michigan, is a popular tourist location. People love to visit the island's famous fudge shops. Because so many visitors buy fudge on the island, tourists are nicknamed "fudgies."

19

Santa gives this recipe two thumbs up. But that's not why these cookies are called thumbprints. To make a bowl in the center of the cookies, you use your thumbs.

DIFFICULTY LEVEL: ★ ★ ☆
MAKES: 3 DOZEN COOKIES
PREHEAT OVEN: 350° FAHRENHEIT

SANTA'S PEANUT BUTTER THUMBPRINTS

WHAT YOU NEED

●● *Ingredients*

½ cup (1 stick) butter
½ cup creamy peanut butter
½ cup sugar
½ cup brown sugar
1 egg
2 teaspoons vanilla extract
⅛ cup milk
1¾ cups flour
1 teaspoon baking soda
red and green colored sugar
1 cup chocolate chips

●● *Tools*

mixing bowl   electric mixer   3 small bowls

baking sheet   oven mitt   pot holder

microwave-safe
bowl

1 In a mixing bowl, add butter, peanut butter, sugar, and brown sugar. Use an electric mixer on medium speed to cream ingredients together.

2 Crack egg into a small bowl and throw away shell. Add egg, vanilla, and milk to the mixing bowl. Mix ingredients with the electric mixer on low.

3 Add flour and baking soda to the mixing bowl. Mix ingredients together on low for 2 minutes.

4 Roll dough into 1-inch balls. Fill one small bowl with red sugar and another bowl with green sugar. Roll dough in red or green sugar. Place dough on a baking sheet, about 2 inches apart. Press your thumb into the center of each cookie to make a small bowl.

5 Bake for 9–10 minutes. Use oven mitts or pot holders to remove baking sheet from the oven.

6 In a microwave-safe bowl, microwave chocolate chips for 40 seconds. If chocolate is not completely melted, microwave an additional 30 seconds. Spoon chocolate into the middle of each cookie. Allow cookies to cool before eating.

Tasty Tip

Peanut Blossoms are another traditional Christmas cookie that combines peanut butter and chocolate. To make these, follow steps 1–5, but don't make thumbprints in the dough. After taking the cookies out of the oven, press a chocolate star in the center of each cookie.

21

On a chilly Christmas morning, nothing warms you up better than a mug of hot cocoa. Double the recipe, and you'll have enough mix to last all winter.

HOLIDAY HOT COCOA MIX

WHAT YOU NEED

•• Ingredients

3 cups powdered milk
½ cup cocoa powder
¾ cup powdered sugar
¾ cup water per mug
1 peppermint candy cane per mug
mini marshmallows

•• Tools

dry-ingredient measuring cups

mixing bowl

mixing spoon

liquid measuring cup

coffee mug

1 Measure powdered milk, cocoa powder, and powdered sugar with dry ingredient measuring cups. Add ingredients to a mixing bowl. Stir ingredients together with a mixing spoon.

2 Measure water with a liquid measuring cup. Pour water into a mug and microwave for 1–2 minutes.

3 Add ¼ cup cocoa mix to the hot water.

4 Stir with a candy cane.

5 Just before drinking, sprinkle a few mini marshmallows on top.

Great Gift Idea

This hot cocoa mix makes a great gift for friends, family, and teachers. Fill a glass jar ¾ full of mix. Fill the rest of the jar with mini marshmallows. Put the lid on tightly. Tie a few candy canes around the top of the jar with colorful ribbon.

It's marshmallow squares with a holiday makeover. Cinnamon candies and green food coloring turn these classic favorites into seasonal snacks.

MARSHMALLOW WREATHS

WHAT YOU NEED

●● *Ingredients*

4 tablespoons butter
1 (10.5-ounce) bag mini marshmallows
3-4 drops green food coloring
3 cups cornflakes
1 cup crisped rice cereal
½ cup mini cinnamon candies

●● *Tools*

microwave-safe bowl

wooden spoon

baking sheet

wax paper
nonstick cooking spray

1 Put butter into a microwave-safe bowl. Heat for 45 seconds or until butter is melted.

2 Add marshmallows to bowl. Microwave for 1 minute. Stir marshmallows with a wooden spoon. Microwave an additional minute or until marshmallows are melted.

3 Add food coloring to marshmallows. Stir with the wooden spoon until marshmallows turn green.

4 Add cornflakes and crisped rice cereal to the bowl. Stir until the marshmallow mixture completely covers the cereal.

5 Line a baking sheet with wax paper. Pour the entire mixture onto the baking sheet. Spray your hands with nonstick cooking spray. Divide the cereal mixture into 6–8 equal parts. Shape each part into individual ring shapes. The mixture will be hot, so you may want to ask an adult for help.

6 Press cinnamon candies on top of wreaths.

25

Tasty Tip

Create the perfect centerpiece by making one big wreath instead of several small wreaths. Just shape the mixture into a large ring. Use a butter knife to cut individual pieces.

Who knew baking cupcakes could be so easy? Just add gumdrops and soda pop. These colorful treats are a fun alternative to fruitcake.

DIFFICULTY LEVEL: ★ ★ ☆
MAKES: 2 DOZEN CUPCAKES
PREHEAT OVEN: 350° FAHRENHEIT

GUMDROP SODA POP CUPCAKES

WHAT YOU NEED

● Ingredients

2 cups gumdrops
1 package white cake mix
1½ cups strawberry soda pop
3 eggs
1 (16-ounce) can vanilla frosting

● Tools

baking cups

muffin pan

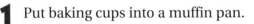
cutting board

kitchen scissors

mixing bowl

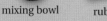
rubber scraper

small bowl

oven mitt

pot holder

1 Put baking cups into a muffin pan.

2 On a cutting board, use a kitchen scissors to cut 1 cup gumdrops into fourths.

3 In a mixing bowl, combine cake mix and strawberry soda pop with a rubber scraper.

4 Crack eggs into a small bowl and throw away shells. Add eggs and gumdrop pieces to the mixing bowl. Mix ingredients together with the rubber scraper.

5 Pour batter into baking cups, filling each ⅔ full. Bake for 20–25 minutes.

6 Use oven mitts or pot holders to remove pan from the oven. Allow cupcakes to cool for 20 minutes.

7 Frost each cupcake and decorate with remaining gumdrops.

Gumdrop Day

In the United States, Gumdrop Day is celebrated on February 15. Invite some friends over to make homemade gumdrops. Just pour powdered gelatin into a bowl. With a straw or an eyedropper, add water to the bowl one drop at a time. After adding seven drops of water, use a fork to scoop out your gumdrop. Roll the gumdrop in sugar and enjoy. Don't forget to serve your guests Gumdrop Soda Pop Cupcakes as they work.

TOOLS GLOSSARY

8 x 8 baking pan — a glass or metal square pan used for baking food

baking cups — disposable paper or foil cups that are placed into a muffin pan to keep batter from sticking to the pan

baking sheet — a flat, metal pan used for baking foods

cookie cutters — metal or plastic shapes that are used to cut cookie dough

cutting board — a wooden or plastic board used when slicing or chopping foods

dry-ingredient measuring cups — round, flat cups with handles

electric mixer — a mixer that uses rotating beaters to combine ingredients

fork — an eating utensil often used to stir or mash

kitchen scissors — a sharp tool with two blades used for cutting food

liquid measuring cup — a measuring cup with a spout for pouring

microwave-safe bowl — a non-metal bowl used to heat ingredients in a microwave

mixing bowl — a sturdy bowl used for mixing ingredients

mixing spoon — a large spoon with a wide, circular end used to mix ingredients

muffin pan — a pan with individual cups for baking cupcakes or muffins

oven mitt — a large mitten made from heavy fabric that is used to protect hands when removing hot pans from the oven

paring knife — a small, sharp knife used for peeling or slicing

pizza cutter — a round knife that spins on a handle as you slice

pot holder — a thick, heavy fabric cut into a square or circle that is used to remove hot pans from an oven

roasting pan — a large, oval pan used for baking a large amount of food

rolling mat — a flat, plastic surface used when rolling out dough

rolling pin — a cylinder-shaped tool used to flatten dough

rubber scraper — a kitchen tool with a rubber paddle on one end

saucepan — a deep pot with a handle used for stovetop cooking

small bowl — a bowl used for mixing a small amount of ingredients

spatula — a kitchen tool with a broad, flat, metal or plastic blade at the end that is used for removing food from a pan

wire cooling rack — a rectangular rack that allows baked goods to cool quickly and evenly

wooden spoon — a tool made of wood with a handle on one end and a bowl-shaped surface on the other used to mix ingredients

GLOSSARY

appetizer (AP-uh-tye-zuhr) — a small portion of food served before or as the first course of a meal

cream (KREEM) — to mix ingredients until soft and smooth

extract (EK-strakt) — a strong solution of liquid made from plant juice; vanilla extract is made from vanilla beans.

set (SET) — to harden

simmer (SIM-ur) — to boil very gently

tradition (truh-DISH-uhn) — a custom, idea, or belief passed down through time

READ MORE

Devins, Susan. *Christmas Cookies!: A Holiday Cookbook.* Cambridge, Mass.: Candlewick, 2007.

Johnson, Kristi. *Peanut Butter and Jelly Sushi and Other Party Foods.* Fun Food for Cool Cooks. Mankato, Minn.: Capstone Press, 2008.

Sindeldecker, Brittany and Erica Sindeldecker. *Just for Kids Cookbook.* Christmas at Home. Uhrichsville, Ohio: Barbour, 2007.

INTERNET SITES

FactHound offers a safe, fun way to find Internet sites related to this book. All of the sites on FactHound have been researched by our staff.

Here's how:
1. Visit *www.facthound.com*
2. Choose your grade level.
3. Type in this book ID **142962017X** for age-appropriate sites. You may also browse subjects by clicking on letters, or by clicking on pictures and words.
4. Click on the **Fetch It** button.

FactHound will fetch the best sites for you!

ABOUT THE AUTHOR

Kristi Johnson got her start in the kitchen when she was a little girl helping her mom, aunt, and grandmas with cooking and baking. Over the years, she decided that her true passion was in baking. She spent many days in the kitchen covering every countertop with her favorite chocolate chip cookies. Kristi attended the baking program at the Le Cordon Bleu College of Culinary Arts in Minnesota. After graduating with highest honors, Kristi worked in many restaurants and currently works in the baking industry.

INDEX